# Awakening Sexy Shakti

## Book I

## A Mystical Journey to Awaken Your Sexuality, Sensuality, Creativity, and Joy

The OM Kitty Series

### Sarah Saint-Laurent

Awakening Sexy Shakti

Cover design by Germancreative

Mandala art design by Greentricks

Publisher: Genesca

Editing by: Abah Mary

Om Kitty® is a Registered Trademark

Printed in the United States of America

# Advance Praise for
# *Awakening Sexy Shakti*
# — Reader's Reviews

*5 STARS ~ If you really want to have some fun while revving up your sacred creative powers, jump on Om Kitty's magic carpet and take a ride. This sacred medicine is just what many of us need: empowerment lessons given with lots of love, humor and lightness. But—reader beware—the miracles that follow might astound you!*

—Sarah Bamford Seidelmann, Author of *What the Walrus Knows* and the highly anticipated *Swimming With Elephants*.

*5 STARS ~ Sarah Saint-Laurent has done it again. Like her first book, Energy Healing Made Simple, she effectively uses the metaphor of "OM Kitty" to beautifully and sweetly guide you to a new realm of inner knowing. Her practical and engaging explanations and visualizations assist you with connecting to your inner knowing, sensuality, and power in a rich and easy to follow way. Her enthusiasm and conviction that we all can awaken to a more full and meaningful life is evident on every page. The steps in her processes compel you to fully embody the teachings, and some of them made me catch*

*my breath with their visceral landing within me. I highly recommend this book, especially if the topic has seemed too difficult or impossible for you. OM Kitty will take your doubts and fears away with her love and charm and steadfast commitment to your heart and happiness.*

—Lauren Oujiri, CoAuthor of *Tenacity & Resolve* and Life Coach at laurenoujiri.com

**5 STARS** ~ I love that Awakening Sexy Shakti explores far more than sexual fire. This book discusses Sexy Shakti as a cosmic feminine-masculine energy, and explores joy, intuition, creativity, as well as sensuality. The three part process is well explained and light-hearted. I also love the resources available, including audio links so you can fully dive into the suggested actions. Om Kitty has a great explanation for using "feeling sensation" in conjunction with visualization which in turn offers a tremendous, simple power to manifesting desired outcomes. Sarah Saint-Laurent has written a practical and easy to follow book that I look forward to sharing with others.

—Amy Colvin, Author of *Cultivating Compassion* and Founder of www.compassionatebalance.com.

*5 STARS* ~ As an author and a dedicated fan of **Om Kitty** and her energy journeys, I must admit I was slightly astonished by Om Kitty's apparent transformation into a sexy siren. Alert—It's not about Om Kitty—This is a delightfully light and vibrant book about awakening your creativity and energy by activating your Sacral Chakra and uniting it with your heart—strength, love and power, just what every women author needs. Interwoven with practical exercises, mystical stories and well-crafted prose, Om Kitty does it again!

What you need, in just the right doses without any woowoo at all—even a supremely practical author like me found value and delight in this entrancing book.

—Susan Jagannath, Author of *The Camino Ingles: 6 days to Santiago*

*5 STARS* ~ '*Awakening Sexy Shakti*, author Sarah Saint-Laurent's second gift to her readers, opens the door to understanding the deep rooted connection between chakras, intention, and manifestation.

Through the eyes and heart of Ms. Om Kitty, we are guided through a process, much of which is based on ancient traditions, that allows an awakening of the heart, mind, and spirit.

The step by step guide, focused on bringing forth the Firebird in each of us, is fascinating in origin and presentation.

Ms. Saint Laurent has mastered the art of teaching her craft in an innovative manner.

There is no doubt following Om Kitty's steps toward the celebration of life, self, and personal growth will bring joy and release to readers.

Well done, Ms. Saint Laurent, on the gifts of *Awakening Sexy Shakti.*"

—Katharine Elliott, Author of *A Camino of the Soul: Learning to Listen When the Universe Whispers* and *Patagonia the Camino Home*

Welcome to the rest of your life!

Hello, my name is OM Kitty, your mystic friend and guide to *Awakening Sexy Shakti*. Let the adventure begin!

Note: Visit http://bit.ly/2jBmE2V-OMKitty-Workbook1 to receive my FREE Essential Companion Workbook. I appreciate having you as a reader and honored member of the Friends of OM Kitty Team.

# Table of Contents

# Introduction

My dear reader ~

If we met earlier because you read my first book **Energy Healing Made Simple—OM Kitty's 8-Day Chakra Activation Journey**, I welcome you back.

If you are new to my book series, I welcome you to my world of **Spiritual Awakening with a *Twist***.

More about me later, but for now I want to say that with this book, it is my honor and sacred duty to help you find and **Awaken Sexy Shakti**.

When you find and awaken Sexy Shakti you will discover tools for living in freedom which will result in becoming UnTamed.

Being UnTamed is explained in detail later in the book. However, in short, it is about waking up every day with the clear understanding that you are truly the master of your destiny. You will be free to live and express yourself and honor your purpose, joy, and bliss. You will be acutely aware that your life and your purpose are entirely in your hands. You will never need the approval of others again. Once you awaken Sexy Shakti—nothing is ever the same . . . because you will be free and UnTamed.

When you are UnTamed, you will create the life you dream of, using your new empowerment coupled with your newly developed intuition, all thanks to awakening Sexy Shakti.

Our goal in awakening Sexy Shakti is to unleash the power of your sensuality, sexuality, creativity, and joy so that you may live your fully awakened, happy, sexy, saucy, and blissful life.

If you want . . .

- to be creative, energetic, and joyful,
- to feel empowered, invincible and blissful,
- to have a deep love, satisfying intimacy, emotional comfort and abundant vitality,
- to be strong, confident and clear,
- to dream big, have no regrets and embrace your true purpose,
- to align with the calling of your Higher Self,

- And, to engage fully in the art of living, unleash your creative genius and squeeze every last drop of happiness out of life . . .

Then I welcome you to your **brave new world**.

Hundreds of years ago, in a different cat-life, I was given a secret, powerful process for self-discovery and transformation and ultimately becoming UnTamed. I call this process **Awakening Sexy Shakti**.

The Awakening Sexy Shakti process teaches you how to live according to your natural intuitive self, your Higher-Self, your wild-ishly free and UnTamed self.

To become UnTamed is to live authentically, to be free of any mask you might wear, any labels you feel weighed down by and to be free of any shackles or chains which may bind you, keeping you small and tethered. Often these shackles are merely thoughts we insist on thinking even though they no longer serve us and sometimes even cause us pain.

When we live in freedom our deepest desires become clear, they become urgent, and they demand to be manifested.

When your Sexy Shakti is awakened, you will naturally live at an entirely different level, releasing the power of your innate sensuality, sexuality, and creativity.

You were destined to find and read this book if you find yourself ever thinking . . .

- Isn't there more to living than just this?
- Where did my fire go? I feel like my inner pilot light has gone out.
- What happened to all my dreams and aspirations?
- I feel completely stuck. God help me! My life has no color, no vibrancy. In fact, sometimes my life seems downright dreary.
- This can't be my real life—my One True Life. Where is all the joy and bliss? Where is are the love and passion . . . and sex?

In fact, you may feel like you are wallowing in a bed of ashes, incinerated, burned to a crisp and about to give up.

You, dear reader, instinctively crave more out of life . . . but you're not sure where to begin. When you awaken Sexy Shakti and learn to become UnTamed, your deepest desires become a reality. Your relationships, work, art, sensuality, sexuality, and creativity will transform because your internal frequency and vibrational level will be at a maximum performance level.

You may have spent a significant amount of time thinking 'If someone could just wave a magic wand to make me feel alive again, everything could be different, everything could be better.'

My friend, you don't need a magic wand. You just need a fun and easy process.

What if you really could reignite your passion and desire for living your One True Life?

Would you do it? (Please say yes. You'll thank me later.)

You intuitively know that thinking about real change, and real transformation is only the 'idea' part. Idea's mean very little without an action plan. Awakening your Sexy Shakti is an action plan which produces change by combining all areas of real awareness development, specifically, the physical, intellectual and spiritual domains.

You want to forge a path to your fully alive and untamed self, and you want it forged from love. You just need some assistance.

**Awakening Your Sexy Shakti** is the process you want. It is a sacred, ancient process and it has been working miracles for a very long time. Now, it is your turn to learn this easy yet life affirming process.

When you activate Sexy Shakti your entire life will change as you usher in vitality, clarity, and friskiness. You will manifest a new sense of confidence—a key aspect of transformation.

My dearest reader, let's be honest, are you craving something deeper and more delicious in your life? My hunch is if you are drawn to this book you don't feel deliciously fulfilled in one or more areas. You likely have a craving to become UnTamed.

Embracing Sexy Shakti is a transformation, in all areas, on all levels and this includes your libido and sexual prowess, which is discussed in more detail in Book II. Each level needs to be activated, and this will usher in the bliss, joy, creativity and the intimate connection you not only crave but require.

You will learn why so many females sadly tromp through their existence, day by day, never discovering how easy and fun it is to live a juicy, sensual, blissful and creatively fulfilled life.

Each part of Awakening Sexy Shakti is designed with you, the reader, in mind. It follows a logical sequence which enables you to quickly grasp the basics of who, what and why Sexy Shakti is important and then builds from there.

No longer will you feel like you are lying in a bed of ashes but instead you will become that famous **Phoenix**, rising from the ashes, transformed, new, fully alive and UnTamed.

<u>In this book you will learn:</u>

- What Sexy Shakti is and why you want to wake it up!
- The benefits of becoming UnTamed.
- The ancient and secret process to awaken Sexy Shakti and transform your life from ho-hum to va va voom.
- True stories (and confessions) of how lives change for the better when you tap into the power and prowess of Sexy Shakti.
- Tips, tricks, and exercises to live your one, UnTamed and joy-filled life,
- How to set ablaze your sensuality, sexuality, and vibrancy,
- And how to ignite your creative genius.

## *Note: A word on becoming UnTamed

To become UnTamed is to live fearlessly and carefree, confidently and unhindered. You live **'wild-ishly.'** You do this by returning to your true nature—which is to fully understand you are a spiritual being inextricably connected to the creative and benevolent power of your Universal Source and therefore, naturally connected to all things. You are more powerful and significant than you realize my dear. You can have, be and do whatever you want . . . and you deserve it. Now you have a process to get it!

When you live UnTamed you live in confidence, you have let go of any fear based mindset, a mindset based on 'lack.'

When you are UnTamed, you let go of any fear of not having enough or not being enough. Have you ever seen a wild lioness wonder about the approval of others? Or a Great Blue Heron worry they weren't enough or didn't have enough? When you are UnTamed you instinctively know there is no lack, you lack nothing, for there is only abundance. You understand this when Sexy Shakti is awake and alive.

When living UnTamed, you live without worry, anxiety or despair. You understand you are entitled to your deepest desires and your desires are part of the true natural process. It is the natural way, the UnTamed way, the way the energy of the universe was designed. The result is you feel alive; you awaken to your naturally inclined, unhindered self. You feel frisky, spontaneous and above all else free. So, you naturally access your greatest level of clarity, joy, sensuality, sexuality, and creativity.

The characteristics of being UnTamed are found in nature and are witnessed throughout the animal kingdom and include:

- Being intimately connected to your Intuition,
- Using your body as an internal GPS system and allowing your physical 'feeling' state to guide you,
- And, allowing your body, heart, and soul to move sensually and freely.

The easiest and most effective process for becoming UnTamed is contained within the ancient process for **Awakening Sexy Shakti**.

# A Special Note
# to the Reader

Dearest Readers ~

If you read OM Kitty's first book Energy Healing Made Simple; you are already aware OM Kitty, ancient sage, mystic, and healer that she is, also represents the wisdom teaching tool of metaphor. OM Kitty is a wisdom teacher, yet she IS a **metaphor**. That is what makes her such an effective teacher. Felines are the perfect metaphor for rebirth and regeneration, having lived nine distinct lives in which to learn and master the art of living.

All great wisdom cultures, Sacred Writings and Texts and enlightened teachers incorporate the use of metaphor. Two prime examples of enlightened teachers using metaphor as a tool would be Jesus Christ and Buddha. In fact, these two great teachers relied on many of the same metaphors, such as fire, water, earth, wind, trees, birds, flowers, and seeds, just to name a few. The use of common beliefs and widely held truths (expressed in the form of a metaphor) make teaching tricky concepts efficient and expedient. A few common examples of widely held beliefs which are often used in metaphors include:

An oak tree grows tall,

A mustard seed is miniscule,

A beautiful lotus grows from the mud.

There is only one reason why metaphor has been so extensively used as a teaching tool, and that is because it works.

Metaphor works quickly and skillfully in explaining difficult or complex concepts. It can be used in a context which is intentionally tailored to meet the level of the audience.

Whether instructing his disciples or teaching large crowds, Jesus Christ masterfully used metaphor. Key examples include:

'The harvest is plentiful, but the workers are few,'

'My yoke is easy and my burden light,'

'Knock, and the door will be opened to you,'

'I am the Alpha and Omega, the beginning and end, the first and the last,'

'The Kingdom of Heaven is like a grain of mustard seed.'

To instruct The Four Noble Truths and The Eightfold Path to Happiness, The Buddha demonstrated his skillful use of metaphor. Examples include:

'The tongue, like a sharp knife, kills without drawing blood,'

'When you like a flower, you just pick it, but when you love a flower you water it daily,'

Of course, there are hundreds of metaphors attributed to these Master teachers.

Please embrace the concept of metaphor as a tool used for clarity when practicing the methods and processes contained in this book.

On another note, I have included real life experiences with the permission of friends, clients or colleagues and peers. However, in every instance, the names and identities have been changed.

I have also included deep research into ancient mystic processes. Please note that Lal Arifa, Raiza, and Jalal are all historical figures and mystics. Jalal is best known as Jalāl ad-Dīn Muhammad Rūmī, or simply just Rumi.

The Tomar Dynasty ruled parts of present-day Delhi and Haryana during 9th-12th century. The history of this dynasty was gathered from traditional medieval bardic legends, which, unfortunately, cannot always be counted on as historically reliable.

Padmaja is a female name meaning born from the lotus or born from the Goddess Lakshmi. I have used this beautiful name for the princess depicted in this writing and for which the processes are attributed.

As in all mysticism and for those on the path of spiritual enlightenment, the intention is key. What you intend while you read this book will affect the result you receive.

I hope my processes will be a welcome part of your regimen in seeking your bliss, diving into your whole, beautiful self and becoming UnTamed while you learn how to find and access your Sexy Shakti.

Namaste.

# Chapter 1

## What Is Sexy Shakti and Why
## Do I Want It Awake?

*"Though it may feel counterintuitive to be this
wild, untamed self, it's actually your truest, most
instinctual experience of being."*

*~ Clarissa Pinkola-Estes,
Women Who Run with the Wolves*

# Chapter 1

# What Is Sexy Shakti and Why Do I Want It Awake?

Sexy Shakti is a secret weapon for creating the most confident, sexy, saucy, fun-filled, UnTamed and wild-ish life imaginable.

This is your LIFE darling, make it count and make it memorable.

Have memorable years, not years that run into each other and are soon forgotten.

Have memorable relationships, memorable intimacy, and memorable laughs.

Create remarkable things, eat remarkable food, have remarkable thoughts.

Enjoy remarkable days, take remarkable trips and be still in remarkable peace and serenity.

'But how OM Kitty?' you ask looking at me with panic stricken eyes.

Fortunately, the process you are about to discover is not only fun and easy but will literally change your life . . . forever.

'OM Kitty, why aren't we naturally following our bliss and enjoying our most content lives?

Darlings, it's not your fault. You've been bombarded with images and talk-bites on pseudo-happiness, the unrealistic and ultimately unsatisfying happiness promoted and displayed 24/7 in magazines, social media, and television. These examples have left many feeling that what they are witnessing is real happiness—but only available to celebrities or the uber-wealthy. This is a sort of *'death by thought-poisoning.'*

The result is many are left believing they are unable to have their deepest desires or achieve heightened experiences of happiness and pleasure because they are lacking in some way; they are not wealthy enough, not attractive enough, didn't attend the right school, don't have the right connections, haven't met the right lover.

That is all a form of brainwashing.

The trick is to understand that you can manufacture the ultimate form of joy, pleasure, and invincibility within the confines of your own miraculous physical body. There is no purchase required, no traveling to endure and no social-media status to check. You simply need to embrace the UnTamed way and Awaken Sexy Shakti.

My hunch is you experience pangs in the center of your chest, the heart energetic center, knowing deeply that there is so much more to life.

You may feel there is a drab veil of mediocrity and dissatisfaction hanging over you as if you are shrouded in a gray mist.

Dr. Clarissa Pinkola-Estes says it well when she writes "Though the gifts of wildish nature come to us at birth, society's attempt to 'civilize' us into rigid roles has plundered this treasure, and muffled deep, life-giving messages of our own souls. Without Wild Woman, we become over-domesticated, fearful, uncreative, trapped."

Does that resonate at all with you dear reader? If you want to read what I consider to be the seminal book on discovering the Jungian Wild-Woman archetype and living in creative and empowered freedom, I enthusiastically refer you to Dr. Pinkola-Este's *Women Who Run With the Wolves*. In my humble opinion, this should be required reading for all females beginning at age 13.

At times, you can peer through this gray mist and see something shiny and sparkling over on the other side. You can just barely make out the fuzzy silhouette that defines what your real life is really meant to be.

The problem is you just can't figure out how to shrug off the God-awful shroud of this imitation-life. You want more, and you want it now. You dearly want to become UnTamed.

I know because there was a time I was in your exact situation. During this desert period, I felt like nothing exciting, joyous or creative would ever be part of my world. I was completely wrong.

You may recall in my first book; *Energy Healing Made Simple*, I explained my absurdly painful first existence, my first cat-life. It was a life shackled to fear based thoughts, over-giving, the care-taking of everyone else but me.

My feminine sensuality was non-existent.

My sexual prowess was in hibernation.

# Awakening Sexy Shakti

My vitality and confidence were missing in action.

My life seemed so very small, insignificant and devoid of any fulfillment. Because I bought into my limiting thoughts and felt unworthy, I made horrible choices in relationships. I endured a senseless, loveless long-term relationship all because I thought I didn't deserve more. So much unnecessary suffering could have been avoided if only I had known about my Sexy Shakti.

There were times when, just like you, I felt the pangs of desire, pangs in my heart where I instinctively knew I was completely missing the point of living. I felt the weight of a drab, misty veil weigh heavily upon my furry shoulders. This misty cloak hid from my personal perspective the richness and fullness which my real life could be.

Then I died.

It wasn't until my second cat-life that I began to pay attention to what my body was feeling and my heart was saying. In my second iteration here I took stock and realized that my life, my thoughts, my actions, are of my choosing and this time I was going to make better choices. Still . . . this was all very new to me, and I stumbled quite a bit. This was before I discovered the power of **Sexy Shakti**.

Obviously, I am a cat, and I have 9 lives. With each successive life, I experience, witness and learn more. That is the bonus available only to felines.

You, my dear, are most likely not of the feline persuasion, and so you do not have 9 lives. You have this one, glorious, delicious life. So you want to get it right, and you want to get it now! You have stumbled upon Sexy Shakti just in time.

You may be asking yourself, 'Is this tiara-wearing, mystic-healer, white Persian Cat the right **teacher** for me?' You might even be thinking 'Who does she think she is anyway, wearing a tiara? Maybe I should just cave into the unhappy, drab, misty veil of a life unlived?'

My beloved friend, there is no better learning tool than a real-time, real-life, in your face **Metaphor**. I am a walking, talking, breathing metaphor for the condition known as 'rebirth.' What you want more than anything else is to 'rebirth' yourself—to come alive and live your best life. Those of the feline persuasion know the magic of 'rebirth,' unlike any others. After all, rebirthing ourselves is our specialty.

And just a side note—I adore my sassy little OM Symbol tiara. Some may think I'm a bit over the top. Some may think I am audacious. They would be right!

I **am** in love with myself. And I had a devil of time learning how to do this. In fact, it wasn't until my third iteration here that I began to clue in strongly to this necessity—and it was not easy. In fact, it was a very uncomfortable learning process at first.

I'll dare to state the obvious—You hopefully understand I am not talking about loving yourself as you stare deeply into a mirror and blow kisses at your own face and taking selfies with your smart phone, then mindlessly reverting back to your compare and despair lifestyle.

I am talking about **truly** loving yourself, the YOU that is intentionally made by Spirit and made of the same beautiful grains of energetic Stardust that compose everything in the cosmos.

This book aims at helping you recognize the **eternal** you that is in direct concert with the Source of All, the infinite field of pure energy and potential. You must learn to love that one, my beautiful friend, perceived flaws and all.

Learning to love the divine within me required a lot of letting go. I had to learn to trust my instinct, give myself permission to allow my deepest desires to matter and look myself in the eye and like what I saw. Learning to truly love all of you, the physical you and the spirit-based you, is no easy party trick.

It requires dedicated practice. It requires personal integrity.

I want you to learn to be in love with yourself. Honestly! It's the only way to approach this life span. When you learn to love yourself the way your Source loves you, magic and miracles will happen.

I love this quote *"There are no extra pieces in the universe. Everyone is here because he or she has a place to fill, and every piece must fit itself into the big jigsaw puzzle."* ~ Deepak Chopra.

You are an integral, necessary piece of the grand plan my dear friend. Please choose to live a memorable life.

I also want you to understand that the seemingly small coincidences you might now be noticing and which you will definitely notice more once you find and awaken Sexy Shakti, are not really coincidences. These are not merely fleeting moments of serendipitous occurrence. Instead, these moments are vibrational. More specifically, what you will begin to notice during this new and seemingly constant rush of 'kismet' is Universal Life Force Energy. You will realize you are in alignment through like-energetic-vibration with the 'Manager' of the cosmos.

When I catch myself standing agog, with my mouth hanging open because I've witnessed yet again another 'miracle' happening in real time, I look up and smile knowing and feeling the undeniable support I am receiving. Sometimes I give the 'Manager' a little wink back letting the cosmos know I'm 'all in' and would like more please.

Deepak Chopra, in *The Spontaneous Fulfillment of Desire: Harnessing the Infinite Power of Coincidence*, writes "Not only are everyday coincidences meaningful, they actually provide us with glimpses of the field of infinite possibilities that lies at the heart of all things. By gaining access to this wellspring of creation, we can literally rewrite our destinies in any way we wish."

"From this realm of pure potential we are connected to everything that exists and everything that is yet to come. "Coincidences" can then be recognized as containing precious clues about particular facets of our lives that require our attention. As you become more aware of coincidences and their meanings, you begin to connect more and more with the underlying field of infinite possibilities. This is when the magic begins. This is when you achieve the spontaneous fulfillment of desire." I love this book and highly recommend it. If you are interested in reading Dr. Chopra's most recent ideas on this subject, you might want to check out *You are the Universe* which I love equally as well.

My dear friend, through each cat life I have learned, loved, lost, lived, gained, matured, honed, and practiced. Do you have any idea how much goes on in 9 life times? The answer is a lot. Through it, all I have studied with masters, including the ones I share in this book, both old and new. It is my honor to share all that I know with you.

One of the most critical lessons I learned was how to awaken my **Sexy Shakti** and become UnTamed. Now it is your turn.

# Chapter 2

# The Energy of
# Sexy Shakti

*"Everything in the Universe has rhythm, everything dances."*

*~ Maya Angelou*


*"What this power is, I cannot say . . .
all I know is that it exists."*

*~ Alexander Graham Bell*

# Chapter 2

# The Energy of Sexy Shakti

Before I share with you the ancient and secret process for <u>Awakening Sexy Shakti</u>, I want to explain the *energy* of **Sexy Shakti**.

The term Sexy Shakti is simply a metaphor I use for awakening and activating the untamed and wild, creative and sensual, *'femasculine,'* life-giving energetic powerhouse of the Sacral Chakra, also known as the $2^{nd}$ Energetic Center.

Are you aware you have the power of a heat-seeking nuclear missile in the core of your 'nether-region'?

Within the vibrant and juicy walls of this sexually charged atomic bomb lives the power to create your blistering hot and joyful life.

**\*Note: Sexy Shakti is a metaphor. It is a term I use to refer to the ancient process of self-discovery and transformation I learned hundreds of years ago. I do not refer here to the energy force associated with the Hindu Goddess Devi nor is this a religious interpretation, and I mean no disrespect to those of the Hindu religion. I am strictly using Shakti as a _term_ to connote a core universal definition of the ultimate 'femasculine' cosmic energy.**

I can tell you that if you truly want to live a fiercely abundant life, the ancient process I call 'Awakening Your Sexy Shakti' works and I'm the proof. So are the others who share their private experiences with you in this book.

You see, what you may not be aware of is that everything that you perceive to be lively, bright, powerful, fierce, sexy, authoritative, happy and creative already resides within you and the focal point dwells within your sacral energetic center.

This _Orange Fireball_ of energetic power is jumping up and down begging to be unleashed. Within these pages, you will learn to easily access your secret power-mojo, deliberately create your most sensual and sexual self, untether your deepest creativity and joy and realize you have the most amazing life to live. This can all be done by learning to how to awaken your Sexy Shakti.

For purposes of this book, Sexy Shakti, as I mentioned above, embodies these **'femasculine'** traits:

- Intuition;
- Boldness;
- Strength and prowess;
- Creative genius;
- Heightened feminine sensuality;
- The supreme feminine creative principal;
- Creation;
- Self-love and self-expression;
- Decisiveness and empowerment;
- And, the definitive nurturing force of the universe.

Carl Jung described the entity known as Shakti as 'My Lady Soul.' Perhaps scholar and author Dr. Clarissa Pinkola-Estes might consider my Shakti metaphor similar to La Loba?

I began using the image of Sexy Shakti in my 3rd cat-life, as a tool to assist me in unleashing all that is powerful and mighty within me. Here you must remember that my first cat-life was rather a disaster. I was without connection to anything spiritual and had no understanding that I am of Source and walk with Source and I am beloved by Source at all times. I was utterly clueless, broken and unable to sense anything magical or energetic within me.

It was my $2^{nd}$ iteration here that I began to clue in. I had an 'awakening' of a sort, but I still had much to learn. At this time I was blessed with fantastic 'introductory' teachers, those beings that come in and out of our lives to bring us contrast and clarity, happiness and frustration. I began to dabble in the spiritual realms and began my journey into mysticism and spiritual awakening. I had a long road ahead.

It wasn't until my $3^{rd}$ cat-life that I fully embraced the inner power I held within my own energetic being. I was blessed to learn an ancient and secret process for becoming untamed and transformed, developed by a master teacher. I share my teacher's 3-part process in this book for the first time.

Through her teachings, I fell deeply and madly in love with the harnessing of my instinctive prowess, my intuition, my creativity, and sensuality. I learned to fire up my 2nd chakra, and I assigned a mental image to this energetic power-house making it my own personal goddess of all things good—Shakti. Who wouldn't want to fall deeply and madly in love with themselves by igniting this powder-keg of empowerment, sensuality and creative genius?

I'm not the first to assign a mental image of the universal power of Shakti. She is often recognized in the form of the Hindu Goddess Devi. I visualize her as the most insanely beautiful, empowered, heroic version of feminine sensuality, nurturing and creative genius I can muster. For me of course, she looks feline. You can envision Shakti as you choose.

## Your Sexy Shakti lives within the Sacral Chakra.

Before we dive into the ancient and prolific process of my teacher, it is a good idea to cover some basic and rudimentary Sacral Chakra knowledge. After all, some readers will be new to energy healing.

In the Sacral Chakra or the 2$^{nd}$ energetic center, dwells the attributes of both the feminine and the masculine. I use the term *'femasculine'* to describe the life-giving energy housed here. Why? The 2$^{nd}$ Energetic Center is anatomically attributed to the reproductive organs of both the male and female.

This energetic center is called the Svadhistana, a Sanskrit term meaning 'the self's dwelling place.'

In the chakra system, the Sacral Chakra is a deep, ripe orange color and the corresponding sound to activate this center is VAM (vummmm).

When concentrating on the Sacral Chakra, I like to vocalize this sound, and in fact, I expand on it. I will purposefully bring my voice register lower and sound out the word Vam, slowly, repeatedly.

After a while, I kick it up a notch by turning Vam (vummmmm) into Va-Va-Va-Vummmmmmm. I do this because I am intentionally setting my mindset for some powerful work.

I want my Sexy Shakti to awaken and be in delight. Va-Va-Va-Vummmmm! I'll show you how to incorporate this into the ancient and secret process further in the book.

I mention I intentionally set my mindset and you can infer that I mean focused concentration combined with intention. This is a theme that runs throughout the entire process you are about to learn. Intention + Focus + Visualization + feeling sensations (emotions) = Fulfilled desires.

It is important to understand the sacral energetic center provides the perfect blending of both the masculine attributes of power, boldness, decisiveness, male centered strength as well as the feminine attributes of creativity, nurturing, sensuality, creation and birth, self-expression, female-centered strength, and self-love.

Dualism is non-existent in the 2$^{nd}$ energetic center. The fusion of these two extremes renders this energetic center a power dynamo for the deliberate creation of joy and bliss. The energy behind your creativity, your sensuality, and your sexuality is unparalleled and is the secret to living your most joyous life.

In short, **Awakening Your Sexy Shakti** is a must; plain and simple. To fully awaken Shakti is to awaken that which is immortal within you fully. Your sacral chakra is a portal to the energy that, and when unleashed, ushers in those tangible, knowable moments of soul alignment.

That is why you want Sexy Shakti awake.

Further, many are aware of awakening Kundalini or Kundalini Rising. You may have even heard that this process is difficult, possibly too esoteric and some even believe potentially dangerous. This book is not about Kundalini.

Instead, it is about the Magical, Mystical, Vibrant, Flaming Orange, Sexy Shakti-Sacral Chakra. This book teaches an easy yet electrifying 3-part process for awakening the cosmic energy that lives within you in order to have a fulfilling creative, sexual, sensual, blissful life. Who doesn't want that? It isn't hard, onerous, esoteric or dangerous. Instead, it is simple and fun.

*Note to Reader: Do you fear awakening your Sexy Shakti is contradictory to your religion or faith practice? I hope this will help you understand that awakening your core sacral life-force has nothing to do with your faith practice. Shakti, as used in this book, is a metaphor. Further, your energetic centers are with you regardless of what your religion or faith practice believes or teaches. You are an energetic being. You are connected to God, Source, Spirit, at all times. Your personal faith tradition need not be altered nor discarded to awaken the divine cosmic energy that lives within you.

My students include Catholics, Episcopalians, Buddhists, Sufi's, Lutherans, Unitarians, Hindu, and everything in between. Awakening Sexy Shakti has nothing to do with religion, so put away any concerns you might have had.

# Chapter 3

# When Sexy Shakti Shook Me

*"Woman is the radiance of God;*
*she is not a creature, she is the creator."*

*~ Rumi*

# Chapter 3

# When Shakti Shook Me

It was the 9th century during the Tomara dynasty, and I resided in Delhi with my mistress and master teacher Princess Padmaja. This is where I began to learn the secret of what I call the **Sexy Shakti**.

Padmaja wore a ruby bindi upon her ajna, her 6th energetic center, known as the 3rd Eye. My princess was a kind and gentle soul, benevolent to all she met. However, it should be known my mistress did not suffer from blind obedience nor was she submissive and silent as many women of her time and locale were.

Padmaja did not allow herself to be disregarded as 'merely' female. She had a magic radiance that exuded authority and wisdom, and she walked with utter confidence. Her voice was strong, and she shared her opinions openly, never fearing she would be silenced or shunned. She swept through the corridors of the palace with an air of freedom and joy.

She was considered to be a sage and wise beyond her years. Her counsel was sought by men and women alike, both high rank and low rank. It was said she had a certain 'knowing,' a connection to the divine, cosmic life force. She treated all she met with the same level of interest and respect.

But her most illustrious trait was her FIRE. She seemed electrified. Her eyes were ablaze with merriment; her smile radiated warmth, her inner conviction was made evident just in the way she walked and moved. She was utterly magnetic.

Padmaja was in complete alignment with her Sexy Shakti, not that she called it this. I was fortunate to learn from Princess Padmaja about this mysterious energy-life-force. My mistress had developed a magical process for harnessing the transformative, energetic power of the Sacral Chakra. She simply called it 'The Process.' Padmaja taught me 'The Process' and how to wield its power and I am eternally grateful.

I sat, intently studying, as Padmaja summoned this life-force-energy. It was part of the very fabric of Padmaja's daily life, and so I made it mine as well. I was mesmerized by her every move, and I missed nothing.

Padmaja began developing her process from the time she was a small girl. She was born a mystic and had always been acutely aware and aligned with her body and the whispers of her soul-self.

Since the process was developed from the 'child's mind' perspective, it is simple, yet abundantly effective. It involves three distinct parts, each separate, yet entangled. Each part may be practiced alone or combined as a complete, intensive practice. Padmaja's process is nothing less than **secret wisdom teachings**, which I now call Awakening Sexy Shakti.

The first part of Princess Padmaja's process concentrated on the sacredness of the Sacral Chakra itself. Padmaja explained that the power of the Sacral Chakra was unparalleled because this energetic center harvests tangible results that can be seen, felt, and heard.

This energy center is the producer of art, song, literature, procreation, human purpose, human desire, intimate relationships, sexual prowess, sensuality incarnate, orgasm, pure, unabashed intimacy, as well as joy, bliss, and gratitude. Therefore, because it 'makes things,' it creates real, palpable 'stuff,' including dreams and desires. Its literal power is incomparable and explosive.

I often refer to the Sacral Chakra as the 'Orange Flame.' It's actually more like an Orange-hued Nitrogen Bomb located in the approximate area of your womb. But mostly I simply call it the dwelling place of **Sexy Shakti**.

As I mentioned, there are three parts to Padmaja's process:

Part 1 involves locating the dwelling place of Sexy Shakti and activating the power of this energetic center. Part 1 is called <u>Igniting the Flame</u>.

Part 2 involves concentrating on the Heart Chakra, the Anahatta—the power seat of love, and uniting, or entangling it, with the Sacral Chakra. This shouldn't surprise anyone who has read my first book.

The vibrant green Heart Chakra is the energetic space between our physical dimension and our spiritual dimension. The Heart Chakra is the portal between earth and heaven. Therefore, it stands to reason that by uniting it with the Sacral Chakra, pure, powerful, transformative alchemy is produced. Part 2 is called Divine Alchemy

Part 3 of Padmaja's process is centered on 'rebirthing' yourself and involves a really big bird. Sounds ominous?

Don't worry; it is a playful way to leap into your physical vitality and creativity through the use of metaphor. 'Rebirth' is release. The product of release is freedom. Freedom is becoming untamed, which unleashes sexual prowess and unabashed sensuality, physical vitality, and clarity. With this accomplished, you can surpass your wildest imaginings. You feel alive, and so all things are possible. Part 3 is called Release of the Phoenix.

Before explaining the processes for awakening your Sexy Shakti it is important that you should know this process is available for **you** right here and right now and is easy to learn and fun.

There is no secret potion to drink or equipment to purchase. And, no travel is required other than leaving the land of your doubts and fear-based thoughts and stepping into the lustrous, spacious land of freedom and joy—your psychic homeland.

Returning now, to my time long ago in India, I took all I gratefully learned from Padmaja and channeled it on a daily basis through deliberately intending to live my most blissful life. I have carried this knowledge with me throughout my various iterations here on this planet. I have cultivated this knowledge, honed it, sharpened it and I now lovingly share it.

Awakening Sexy Shakti is about becoming **UnTamed**.

It is about becoming wild-ish once more. Originally, we were all wild-minded, wild-acting, wild-loving, free, untethered, loose and frisky, for we were of Spirit, and we still are. You are a pure energetic being. Unfortunately, the world has a way of making us forget who we really are. My role is to help you remember.

It is imperative you reclaim *The Wild You* as in experiencing first-hand, the Divine Wild Woman archetype, the abode of wild selfishness (yes, you read that right—you need to learn to be Self-*ish*— meaning be about the self for a while. Believe me, everyone will continue to muster on—even without your self-perpetuating care-taking . . . trust me.)

Awakening Sexy Shakti will allow you to protect the sacred ground of your psychic homelands like a Goddess-Knight with one impeccable quest, one sacred charge and that is diligently reclaiming your wild, untamed, creative, sensual, sexual, blissful self and protecting your psychic homeland.

A great article dedicated to this exact proposition can be found at www.saintlaurentcoaching.com/wild-woman/lost-intuition, which you can read at your leisure.

I also like to share other sources of inspiration whenever possible. In a lovely book written by Heather Ash Amara entitled *Warrior Goddess*, the author shares, "If you don't love and honor yourself with every fiber of your being, if you struggle with owning your power and passion, if you could use more joyful play and simple presence in your life, then it is time for an inner revolution. It is time to claim your Warrior Goddess energy."

I couldn't agree more. And in my opinion, the best way to go about doing just that is finding and awakening Sexy Shakti.

Reader, please note there is an important thread that runs through each of the three parts of the Awakening Sexy Shakti process. Each part requires you to set an intention and to become familiar with the art of visualization. Setting an intention, becoming the emotional 'feeling state' of that intention and combining it with focused visualization will facilitate deliberate creation. You want to deliberately become UnTamed and awaken Sexy Shakti.

Let's begin!

# Awakening Sexy Shakti

## – Part One –

## Igniting the Flame

# Chapter 4

# Getting Prepared

*"Dance, when you're broken open. Dance, if you've torn the bandage off. Dance in the middle of the fighting. Dance in your blood. Dance when you're perfectly free."*

*~Rumi*

# Chapter 4

# Getting Prepared

**What you will need:**

- A comfortable place to sit in silence.
- Pre-selected rhythmic music of your choice. I am attracted to sensuous eastern music. I also like to use primal drum beat music, and I like a good Tango. I want music that makes me feel on fire, sensual, beautiful, wild, free and possibly out of control. *
- Room to dance and stomp.

*Music selection samples:

Music 1 (compiled by BMC) –
www.youtu.be/jNbr9vyUQm4

Music 2 (Aiden Jaan – Kali Taal) –
www.youtu.be/msxaObFAsYE

Music 3 (Drumming – harem belly dance –
Darbuka) – www.youtu.be/8T-
aTqQPMhU?list=PL711FC9BA87279C10

Music 4 (Gotan Project Tango – Santa Maria de
Buenos Aires (Del Buen Ayre) –
www.youtu.be/80hIlfwh3Zc

Music 5 (Armik – Tango Flamenco) –
www.youtu.be/ivgjXnz8oZo

Music 6 (Tina Turner – Sarvesham Svastir Bhavatu
– Peace Mantra) – www.youtu.be/jpux0kU4DYI


Following are the five steps that comprise Part One
– Igniting the Flame.

# Chapter 5

# Step 1 – Finding Sexy Shakti

Our Sacral Chakra is the dwelling place of our Orange Flame. From this flame, we reignite our soul through our capacity for desire, creation and personal relationships.

# Chapter 5

# Finding Sexy Shakti

### Step 1

Princess Padmaja's process begins with silence. Silence allows the small tender voice of the soul to be heard. Listen intently in silence and begin to simply . . . remember. Begin to recall. Who is that beautiful soul that arrived here? Recall the eternally beloved being that you really are. Soon you will hear the inner voice whispering . . . 'welcome home.'

Please don't doubt the inner voice for it is a song of recognition. Your inner wisdom is speaking . . . it is your Higher Self, the one who never forgot your origin and your purpose.

The words are whispered . . . 'Love yourself first, create your art, dance your jigs, light your lamps, heal yourself first . . . and ignite your internal flame.'

Now that you have been in silence for just a bit and are listening to the Inner-Siren, your rekindled soul-spark whispering words of truth, you will draw your attention **inward** and **downward**.

In the center of your abdomen, approximately two inches below your navel lies the cynosure of the Sacral Chakra—its **Hot Spot**.

Your goal is to make contact with the cynosure. The path to travel in order to arrive at this **Hot Spot** is your vaginal cavity.

You are going to use two muscles, your brain, which is your thinking muscle and your vaginal muscle. You will use your thinking muscle to visualize while you use your vaginal muscle in the physical act of traveling to the domain of Sexy Shakti.

Mentally travel to your vaginal canal.

Set an intention. Your intention might be 'I want to be UnTamed, to live wildly, passionately and effortlessly,' or 'I want to be intimately aware of my innate power.' Another example of an intention might be 'I intend to find my personal power-house and unleash my intuitive prowess.'

Begin by tightening your vaginal wall. You want to know, without a doubt, your vaginal walls are intact, strong and powerful. Sometimes I find it is helpful to imagine a fuzzy, bright orange ball sitting smack dab in the middle of the vaginal cavity. My goal is to deflate this ball using my brain muscle by visualizing in concert with my vaginal muscles.

As you 'crush the orange ball,' concentrate on squeezing the walls together. Begin to lift and raise the muscle to its maximum height by squeezing the walls inward and upward.

Hopefully, you have crushed your orange ball to smithereens. You know without a doubt your vaginal muscles are working. Bravo!

Now I want you to imagine your vaginal canal as a cave. Your goal is to reach the apex of the cave.

You don't want to reach the back of the cave as that leads nowhere and is a dead end. Instead, you want to locate the apex of the cave, which is up, up, up. That is the location of the cynosure of the sacral chakra. That is Sexy Shakti's Hot Spot. It sits internally, centered, approximately two inches below your navel. That is where you want to go. That is your destination.

Exploring caves is called Spelunking. As you 'spelunk' your way through the cave, on your journey to make contact with the Hot Spot, attempt to stay focused but remember to have fun. There is no sense awakening Sexy Shakti if the journey isn't a fun experience.

To reach the apex, continue to concentrate on tightening the walls of the cave. Feel into this sensation and imagine the walls of your cave can crush granite boulders. You are now beginning to experience the physical location of this energetic center.

That is another miracle of the sacral chakra. The $2^{nd}$ energetic center harvests tangible results which we feel, see and hear. No other energy center is capable of this particular form of creation—the 'making of tangible stuff' so to say. You are truly able to feel this flaming orange chakra. Remember to breathe throughout the process. If you hold your breath that will only make you dizzy. You don't want to be dizzy when spelunking.

The tighter and higher you take this action, the stronger you will feel into the Hot Spot of the $2^{nd}$ Chakra. Take this sensation as high as you can manage. When you are convinced, you have reached as high as possible, congratulate yourself. You have reached your destination. But your 'cave' exploring has just begun.

Now if this sounds similar to a Kegel you would be right . . . and wrong. This is an activation process, not a gynecological exercise. Instead, think of this as the **Mother of All Kegels**.

You will hold and squeeze for a prolonged period. You are also setting an intention, and you are visualizing. This is not performing Kegels. This is a magical process to ignite your **Sexy Shakti** and fire up your Sacral Chakra.

Concentrate on the apex of your cave. Tighten the walls of the cave and hold this squeeze for at least 30 seconds, 60 seconds if you're able.

Feel into this sensation with all the power you can muster. Recall the intention you have set. Breathe in deeply through your nose and exhale slowly through pursed lips. You are igniting your flame. In fact, you are setting it ablaze.

Just for the heck of it, see if you can bring the apex of the cave, the Hot Spot, even higher. You might be surprised how much further, higher, and deeper you can go with practice.

* Note: Step 1 is going to be an essential element when we get to Awakening _Your_ Sexy Shakti—Book

II, which I have developed and based upon Princess Padmaja's principles, which deals exclusively with the subject of becoming the Master of Your Sexual Dominion. First, you must learn the location of the Hot Spot. So dear friend, get to know this area intimately. Make it your new favorite destination.

*Another Note: For the males, feline and human alike, you too can access this feeling sensation. Visualize your own cave and go spelunking. Bring your attention inward to the same location described above, approximately two inches below your navel. Imagine that you are cutting off your ability to void (urinate) by internally ceasing that function. You too are more or less at the cynosure or **Hot Spot** for the male counterpart.

Now that you understand how to make contact with Sexy Shakti physically it is time for a little mental visualization which involves a bit of mystical traveling.

# Chapter 6

## Step 2 – Divine Travel

## Finding Your Sacred Space

# Chapter 6

# Divine Travel – Finding Your Sacred Space

## Step Two

Focusing your attention on your Hot Spot, mentally bring yourself into a virtual place of nature.

Visualize your most idyllic natural setting. For some it will be the woods, others will be at the sea-shore; others will find themselves in a field of daffodils.

Let your visualization take you to the tallest mountain peak, or a dark, velvety forest copse or perhaps a perfectly positioned rock-cropping jutting out of a silent desert. Whatever natural setting brings you complete happiness and peace—please mentally go there.

While in your idyllic place of nature, maintain your connection with the Sexy Shakti. With focused mental attention, lower yourself to your hands and knees and visualize digging into the wet earth (or dry sand, or cool grass, etc.) with your hands.

Feel the particular physical sensation of your idyllic place in nature. You are digging; your hands are getting dirty, you smell the dirt, loam, grass, mud, heather . . . whatever the ground is which you are currently digging.

You've now dug a tunnel. Mentally begin to crawl on your hands and knees into your tunnel. You crawl deeper. Visualize this tunnel as being narrow and dark, only wide enough to fit your body snugly.

You travel along on your hands and knees feeling the coolness and dankness of the tunnel as it envelops your body. You notice the utter silence. You are only aware of the sound of your heart and the rhythm of your breathing.

In the silence, you are able to notice that your breathing and heart beat are in sync. This brings an unexpected sense of happiness. You understand that everything is connected. You notice everything is working the way it is meant to work. You begin to feel the magical aspect of 'Oneness.' You inherently know that you, your physical apparatus, your soul, the universe, are all in sync and connected.

You continue crawling along in your tunnel in silence. Suddenly, you see a small fissure just ahead. It is a small crack allowing a glimmer of light to seep in. As you move slowly forward, the crack grows larger. As you reach the end of the tunnel, the crack has transformed into a portal.

This portal seems magical. It appears as a shimmering wave of energy.

Because you feel a sense of wonder and anticipation, you gently crawl through the portal. Amazed and excited, you see you have popped up into a clear, open space and you stand and look around.

What space are you in? Is it a grassy field? Are you standing on a mossy mound high on a cliff overlooking a vast ocean? Is it an open spot among a copse of alders? Is this a space in a darkened jungle with a large, flat boulder to sit upon? Where are you?

Take a moment to visualize this sacred spot. You have just energetically conjured your private, sacred nature-den. Often, this place looks nothing like the idyllic nature space you just traveled from. Many times, in visualization, we end up in a place that is unlike anything we've imagined before. This new place is a sacred spot.

This is a place you can return again and again because now it exists in your psyche. Your soul has conjured this sacred place—this is now **your place**. You will be able to return to this place whenever you want to instantly access stillness and ground yourself.

Begin to listen. What do you hear? Is there a brook babbling, or jungle creatures making soft sounds? Is there a soft breeze blowing through the tree canopy above?

When you look around, do you spy any little beasties? Are there any small creatures peering back at you? If yes, what do you see? Is there a lovely mother spider dangling from a silky thread? Perhaps there is a baby hedge-hog poking its head out of a small hole, or a school of koi fish circling a pond or a black raven watching you inquisitively.

The first time I traveled to my newly conjured sacred spot I was met by a black panther. This animal totem has been with me ever since. Whenever I travel to my nature-den, the panther is there to welcome me. Then she leaves me to sit in silence and focus on the process of grounding in my sacred spot.

*Many who have worked with me have benefited from my assistance in guiding them through the process of visualizing the sacred domain described above. You can access my guided meditation to visualize a sacred nature spot in the resource section if you feel so inclined.

# Chapter 7

# Step 3 – 'Grounding' in Your Sacred Place

# Chapter 7

# Grounding in Your Sacred Place

### Step 3

Your newly conjured sacred-space is specifically designed for you to learn the technique of grounding. It is important to learn to ground in order to ignite the flame of Sexy Shakti.

Grounding incorporates the principles of mindful awareness, and the easiest and fastest way to achieve mindful awareness is by focusing on our breath. This is called Mindful Breathing.

Begin by breathing in deeply through your nose for the count of 6 and gently out through pursed lips for the count of 6. I like to visualize I am gently blowing out a puffy dandelion. Repeat this breathing process four times.

See yourself standing in your conjured sacred-space. Spread your legs hip-width and push your feet into the ground. Place your hands on your hips. Bring your shoulders back and lift your chest. Relax your neck, throat, shoulders and facial muscles.

Feel your feet pressing into the earth. Imagine vines are sprouting from your feet, and they travel into the ground of this sacred place anchoring you to the center of the earth.

You feel solid and supported.

Attempt to listen intently. Be as still with your breathing as possible. Remain grounded. Remain in concert with Sexy Shakti knowing you are connected physically. Remind yourself you are connected by giving Shakti another tight, deep, squeeze.

Now that you have grounded and you are connected to Sexy Shakti, and you are comfortably situated within your favorite natural setting you can begin to intentionally focus on deliberately creating your desires.

# Chapter 8

## Step 4 – 'Feeling' Your Desires

# Chapter 8

# Step 4 – 'Feeling' Your Desires

### Step 4 – 'Feeling' Your Desires

Igniting the flame that is Sexy Shakti produces the manifestation of desires. Your desires are real things which can be held, smelled and ingested. They aren't theories. They are real. You can experience a desire through the use of your 5 senses.

A critical component to Part 1 of Padmaja's process is learning the correct way to create your desires deliberately.

You now know how to locate the cynosure or the Hot Spot of your Sacral Chakra.

The second step is visualizing and then 'traveling' to your favorite place in nature and conjuring your personal sacred space.

The third step is to ground in this sacred natural setting, feeling solid and supported. You have become mindful and aware through the art of mindful breathing.

We now come to the fourth step in Part 1, which is to create the feeling sensation associated with the desired outcome. You begin with intentional focus which you are already poised to do now that you have found your cynosure, conjured a sacred nature den and grounded yourself in the state of awareness.

Desires are created through intentional focus and visualization. Once you are able to intentionally focus and visualize your intended outcome, it is essential that you **become** the feeling sensation associated with the desired outcome.

If your desired outcome is to manifest joy and creativity, you will need to **become** the feeling of joy and creativity. Padmaja was always very clear and adamant about this point. Becoming the feeling sensation of your desire is essential.

This is often where a hint of resistance pops its little monkey head up.

Often I hear participants in my Sexy Shakti training say 'Look OM Kitty—I'm fine with visualizing and focusing on what I want. But becoming the feeling sensation? That just sounds nuts.'

I then need to reiterate the basic Rule #1 in the deliberate creation playbook.

**Rule #1 of the Deliberate Creation Playbook—** reads as follows:

**Become the Feeling Sensation of your Desire.** Do not continue with the Deliberate Creation Playbook until completing Rule #1

You become the feeling sensation of a desire by recalling what it felt like to experience a similar desire.

You will be unable to manifest a desire if you cannot conjure the associated feeling of already having experienced the desire. There is no way of getting around this—Finito, over-and-out, period.

Have you attempted to manifest your little tush off and nothing has happened?

You think about lovers, jobs, travel, affluence, belongings, peace, serenity and success and you silently, or even openly, beg for these desires to materialize.

You prevail upon the angels to come to your aid.

You make pacts with God.

You share your intended desires with friends, colleagues, life-coaches, anyone who will listen, yet nothing really ever happens?

Are you interested to know why?

The reason you are not manifesting all that you intentionally desire is that you have not lined up your desires with the correlating 'feeling sensation.' You must become the 'feeling sensation' of that which you desire.

## True Story #1:

Here is an example of someone who worked with me in Sexy Shakti training. I'll call her Antonia for confidentiality purposes.

Antonia was intrigued and eager to learn Princess Padmaja's process. She participated enthusiastically. She took notes, and she diligently practiced all the steps without reservation.

However, Antonia was severely challenged by Step 4 of Part One. She couldn't wrap her head around becoming the feeling sensation of her desire.

Antonia deeply wanted to have the mate of her dreams, and together they would live in a spectacular home on a large corner lot, produce 4 little Antoia's and live happily ever after as she composed lyrics for songs and made a lot of money. She had practiced manifesting her desires for several years (or so she thought) on her own. She was extremely **focused**.

It was an epic fail. None of Antonia's deep desires materialized. Antonia had focused herself right on to her knees sobbing in her bedroom countless nights, lying awake, losing sleep and failing to deliver her song lyrics to purchasing customers.

She was so **focused**; she forgot to eat. She made fantastic deals with the powers that be. She experienced episodes of intermittent depression. She felt an underlying anxiety much of the time. She noticed her hair was thinning and her fingernails were brittle and chewed to the quick.

Through her personal training on Sexy Shakti, Antonia eventually realized she had everything backward.

Allow me to ask you this question, when a general feeling of constant anxiety exists, accompanied by a physical sensation of butterflies zooming around your chest cavity, while you bite your nails, pace the floor, with no desire to eat or sleep, is it reasonable to expect that the universe will produce a silver platter and lavishly serve up your wildest dreams?

You know this answer already, right? Surely you've read the countless books that have been written on the Law of Attraction and understand why this doesn't work? Correct?

What's that you say? You've never read about the 'feeling sensation' in any of the books written on Law of Attraction and manifesting? Yes . . . actually, I already knew that.

My question is why do they keep leaving this little nugget out? You can't 'wish,' beg and suffer for desires my dear darlings. It doesn't work like that.

In fact, Antonia's behavior described above is a clear contradiction to the smooth sailing of the *SS Law of Attraction Luxury Liner*. She was poised to fail, poor little darling. She didn't have the right book or the right process.

You must **become the feeling sensation** of the desired outcome. If you want creativity and joy, you must be the feeling of creativity and joy. You must **be the experience** of creativity and joy.

How do you do this? Simply by remembering a time you experienced creativity. Then you remember a time you experienced joy. It's as simple as that my lovelies. No need to manipulate this into some giant hairball.

If your desired outcome is bliss and sensuality you proceed as follows:

1. Recall a time you experienced bliss.
2. Recall a time you experienced sensuality.

'Hold it right there OM Kitty. I've never felt bliss or sensuality!'

I respond, 'Ahem . . . yes, you have."

You have experienced your interpretation of bliss or sensuality, your own personal baseline of bliss and sensuality. What is your 'normal'? In other words, you may not have experienced what you *imagine* bliss and sensuality to be in their ideal state, but there has been a time where you have experienced 'bliss–for-you' and 'sensuality-for-you.'

It does not matter that others may deem your normal baseline for bliss and sensuality to be complacency or abject boredom. It is your personal-normal. It represents the happiest you've ever been, or the most luxuriously satisfied.

This is where you **start**. Begin by identifying the baseline feel-good sensation that generates the closest proximity you can recall to the feeling sensation of bliss and sensuality, or creativity and joy, etc. And then we build on that.

Do you recall the old saying 'One man's feast is another man's famine?' Perhaps you've never felt bliss, as you interpret it to be, so you believe you are at a disadvantage and cannot conjure the feeling sensation to manifest your desires.

But I say yes, you have had your own personal interpretation of bliss. Maybe you didn't win the lottery, or sail a yacht around the world, or visit the Himalayas, or even land the job of your dreams. So what? What if having a soft pillow under your head at night when you go to sleep is your biggest dose of bliss? Then I say **START** there!!!!

Don't worry—everyone and everything needs a starting point. With deliberate creation, it won't take long to see the level of feeling sensation increase dramatically as you begin to attract more of what you desire. The momentum begins, and then the cycle continues. Soon you will be baffled as to why it took you so long to catch on to this quantum reality.

Think about the following partial list of desired outcomes and give consideration to where your own-personal-normal lines up. Remember—STOP judging yourself!

Creativity;

Joy;

Empowerment;

Invincibility;

Bliss;

Sexual fulfillment;

Sensuality;

Vitality;

Confidence;

Clarity.

Allow yourself to become aligned with **your** feeling sensation for any or all of these desires. Begin now. Make this process light and fun.

If your inner, UnTamed, Higher-Self is telling you that creativity is the road to your personal bliss, recall a time when you were utterly happy while being creative.

Perhaps it is simply recalling a time in kindergarten when you cracked open that new box of 64 Crayola Crayons. Remember that feeling? Remember that smell? Can you recall all those magical sticks of colored wax just waiting for your little fingers to make a masterpiece? You were the master of your dominion—you felt invincible.

That is the feeling sensation we are going for. Try this experience with the entire list above. You have a personal experience with each of these desired outcomes.

You can access my tool to further develop this practice on the resource page.

Darling—I know you can do this.

# Chapter 9

# Step 5 – Move It Like Your Life Depends On It!

*"To dance is to be out of yourself, larger, more powerful, more beautiful. This is power, it is glory on earth, and it is yours for the taking."*

*~ Agnes de Mille*

# Chapter 9

# Move It Like Your
# Life Depends On It

Step 5 of Padmaja's process incorporates the power of dance.

Sexy Shakti loves to stomp and gyrate, swivel and swirl, flow and release. Pick one or all of the music suggestions mentioned at the beginning of Part One and start moving. Feel free to find your own music choice. I just make a small suggestion that it be sensual, sexy, and primal. Once in a while incorporate music that contains drumming.

When beginning Step 5, always reconnect with the Hot Spot. Deliberately focus on the cynosure where Sexy Shakti is ready and waiting. Set ablaze the fire that is Shakti. Begin by grounding your feet into the floor. Breathe in deeply. Lift your chest upwards, open your shoulders.

Start by swirling your hips. The key here is wild abandon.

You've heard the saying 'Dance as if no one is looking'? Do it. Do it now. There are no directions here. Just dance. And stomp your feet if you can. I always find this helps create a ferocious sense of power within me. Be sexy and sensual darling. No one's watching. Dance for at least 20 minutes a day if at all possible and more if you can and love the way you feel afterward.

Listen friends—I get downright erotic when I dance. I hope you will do the same. Dance by yourself if you feel self-conscious. Believe me; there is nothing more empowering than dripping with sweat as you heat up your Sacral Chakra while gyrating the mother-loving socks out of your hips. It is absolutely amazing. It is freeing, and it is so damn good for you. Please practice this 5th step as often as you can.

Last bit of advice on Step 5—Don't over-think it. Have some fun.

Look at all you have just accomplished. You know the resting place of Sexy Shakti. You have activated your Sacral Chakra. You have traveled to a sacred place and have become grounded, setting an intention for a desired outcome, and have aligned with the feeling sensation. You have set Shakti ablaze through music and dance.

It is now time to show gratitude to Sexy Shakti. Before we move on to Part 2 of the Process of Awakening Sexy Shakti, we pause and acknowledge the tools and awareness we have just accessed. You have made a quantum leap my friend. Offer gratitude and embrace the feeling sensation of gratitude. Place your hands over the area of your Sacral Chakra and close your eyes. Breathe. Smile.

### True Story #1—continued:

Remember my student, Antonia, I mentioned above?

Antonia needed a lot of work accessing the 'feeling sensation' of her dream life. She had never intentionally conjured a feeling sensation in her life. She isn't alone. How often do you intentionally choose to conjure a feeling sensation to manifest your dreams? Hopefully, you now understand the importance of this little nugget of wisdom.

Antonia and I worked for quite a while together. The number one game changer for Antonia was Step 5. Dancing in a focused, deliberately freeing manner, allowed Antonia's Sexy Shakti to ignite in a way that she could have only dreamed about. Antonia incorporates Steps 1-5 into her routine on a weekly basis. But she practices Step 5 every day.

The physical moving of her body in a sensuous, wild way allowed Antonia to become connected to her body for the very first time. She embraced the feeling of wild abandon, and her imagination began to soar. It became easy for Antonia to imagine and become the feeling sensation of her desires.

Antonia now maintains a 'tight grip' on Sexy Shakti, regularly swinging her hips, undulating and flowing with the intent on sparking her imagination and igniting her internal flame. Antonia is now a master at manufacturing the feeling sensations necessary to manifest her dreams desires.

I am happy to report that Antonia is happily situated exactly where she wants to be and has managed to get her spouse involved in gyrating with her. Her three babies are happy dancers too.

# – Part Two –

## Divine Alchemy ~
## Combining the Heart
## and Sacral Chakras

# Chapter 10

## Divine Alchemy

## Combining the Heart and Sacral Chakras

*"You are the master alchemist. You light the fire of love on earth and sky, in heart and soul of every being."*

~ *Rumi*

# Chapter 10

# Divine Alchemy ~ Combining the Heart and Sacral Chakras

The Anahatta or Heart Chakra is a powerful counterpart to activating your Sacral Chakra. The Heart Chakra is the 4th energetic center. In this physical world, the concept of the number 4 is prevalent and very important. 4 is the geometry of a square. The heart contains 4 chambers.

There are 4 elements—Earth, Air, Water, and Fire.

We have 4 states of matter. Solid, gas, liquid and, plasma.

There are 4 seasons, winter, spring, summer, and autumn.

There are 4 directions, North, East, South, and West.

The Four Elements of this physical world are interconnected in a myriad of ways.

Earth aligns with the physical realm, the solid state, winter, North, and food.

Air aligns with the mental or intellectual realm, the gas state, spring, East, and oxygen.

Water aligns with the emotional realm, the liquid state, summer, and the Southern direction.

Fire aligns with Spirit—the most important and often overlooked element for the igniting of spiritual consciousness and awakening Sexy Shakti. Fire aligns with the plasma state, autumn, West, and Prana.

The 4th energetic center or Heart Chakra is the power seat of **Love** and works similarly to a portal. It sits directly between the lower three chakras of the earthly plane and the higher three chakras of the spiritual realm. It is the conduit between divinity and humanity.

*Note: If you find you could benefit from understanding the entire chakra system better, there are many good books on the subject, including my first book.

Divine Alchemy occurs when the power of the Heart Chakra and Sacral Chakra are combined.

In part two of Padmaja's process, which I call Divine Alchemy, you will witness the magical chemistry of combining the abode of creativity, sensuality, and desire with the power seat of unconditional love and compassion. It is a powerful combination.

Part two of Padmaja's process contains 3 easy steps, and they are set out individually below.

But first, I want to share the following information. The Heart chakra is the doorway to an unbounded, joyful connection with the Universal Source of All.

We know all material creation, the things which are tangible to us through our 5 senses, are comprised of the same elements. All and everything is made by the same One Great Source. This 'Source'—God—Higher Power—Spirit—The Universe—this source is the unified field. Within this unified field exists everything and everything is comprised of this unified field. Think of this field as the One Great Beloved—the Source of All.

We live, breathe, eat, speak, touch and move through this benevolent field of energetic perfection. The key to awakening Sexy Shakti and living an UnTamed life is to understand that our abundance comes from this very field of potentiality. Our abundance is present and waiting to be summoned.

Your desires combined with the inherent potentiality that lays waiting in this field of pure cosmic energy are ripe for the picking. The One Great Beloved is waiting for you to believe in yourself and trust that you are a beloved aspect of this field of potentiality.

The Divine Alchemy of the Heart and Sacral Chakra combination is exquisite energy. It is orgasmic energy. It is the energy exposed when you are rapturously blissful when you are overtaken with gratitude when you feel supremely loved or understood. This energy of combining the Anahatta and the Svadhisthana is the penultimate emotion of completeness, oneness, and belonging. Now, let's explore Divine Alchemy—Part Two of Padmaja's process.

# Chapter 11

## Step 1 Visualization Meditation ~ Feeling Grateful

# Chapter 11

# Step 1 Visualization Meditation ~ Feeling Grateful

We begin Step 1 by setting an intention for a desired result. We then incorporate the powerful feeling sensation of being grateful.

Consider what it is you want more of in your life—more love, closer relationships, better health, financial freedom, an artistic outlet to develop your creative genius. They are all linked to creation—which is empowered through the Sacral Chakra. Setting an intention is critical, and visualization will assist you in Step 1.

In this process, you will be utilizing the power of both the Sacral Chakra and the Heart Chakra. The Anahatta, or 4th energy center, has the energetic power of a jet-propulsion booster-rocket. You, my friend, are ready for Lift Off!

Whatever it is you most desire, allow your mind to form a clear intention. Feel free to make your intention an UnTamed Life. It can be as simple as 'I want to live the UnTamed Way!' Or, it could be 'I want to become UnTamed and joyous!' However, it is important that you always make the intention something that powerfully resonates with you.

Plant the seed of this intention and give Sexy Shakti a hug at the cynosure.

Remain connected to Sexy Shakti and concentrate clearly on your intention.

Now visualize the vibrant, life giving color green of the Anahatta wash over your sacral chakra. Cocoon your Hot Spot in a soft blanket of emerald green and feel the universal power of pure love seep into your domain of creation.

In a peaceful, mindful way, say to yourself, 'I create my abundant, creative, and joyous life through the power of love and the support of my infinite Source.'

Visualize your intention. If your intention is to live an Untamed Life, what does that look like to you? Picture it—are you eager, happy, feeling light hearted, playful, spontaneous, creative, sexual, sensual, secure and empowered?

Now that you have visualized your intention it is essential to affirm your intention.

It is unfortunate that affirmations are often considered by some, to be nothing more than silly mumbo-jumbo. That, my friends, is an uninformed viewpoint and big mistake.

The science of neuroplasticity has proven the efficacy of affirmations. Affirmations literally retrain and rewire your brain. The science of rewiring your brain isn't complex, but it deserves a fully fleshed-out explanation. I will be publishing a book on the science of brain rewiring in the near future. For now, be sure to download my free gift I mention at the beginning of the book for a primer on neuroplasticity. It is a token gift of appreciation to you from my heart. You can access this FREE download by visiting http://bit.ly/2jBmE2V-OMKitty-Workbook1.

Practicing affirmations daily and with frequency will intrinsically change the energy of your soul. I offer the affirmations below, designed to rewire your brain and create a powerful change in your everyday reality.

That which we project through affirmation becomes the basis of our awareness and creates permanent changes. Make these affirmations a part of your daily routine. Or, make your own personal affirmations. In any event, please affirm!

- I am awake!
- All is perfect—I am perfect—just as I am, at this moment. All is well.
- I am grateful. I shout my gratitude!
- I choose to be outrageously thankful and fall in love with the knowledge that I am eternally loved.
- I am empowered.
- I feel bold knowing this new reality. I am limitless. My soul is fearless.
- Today, in this moment, I fear not.
- I let go of my projected fear. I choose a new self-image.
- I am whole.
- I come from Love.
- I've got this . . . I am supported.

- I follow the OM Kitty way, the UnTamed way, the Sexy Shakti way. I have nothing to fear. There is nothing to fear. Fear is an illusion. I am OK with uncertainty. I feel free.

How does that feel? Those are some powerful affirmations.

You have visualized your intention, and you have affirmed your soul's desires.

It is now time to establish the feeling sensation of being grateful.

The emotional feeling sensation of gratefulness is so powerful it will cause miracles in your life. It is powerful enough to prevent and even stop wars. You want this powerful feeling sensation because it fills you with energy so pure and strong that nothing can get in its way.

Bring to mind something you are truly grateful for. Is it your luxurious mane of hair, your new mystery novel, your pet, your down comforter?

My friend Rachel usually uses her 'go-to' gratefulness gizmo—Rachel is grateful for her Spotify Music App. Nothing fills her with a clean sense of gratefulness, free from contrast, like Spotify.

That is an important distinction, my friend! Please note the following:

When entering into a state of 'feeling' emotion,' please be careful that the subject isn't actually a two sided sword. It won't help feeling grateful you are married rather than single if your marriage is riddled with a long list of complaints. It won't help feeling grateful for your car if you can't afford to fill up the gas tank. It is important to find 'clean' feelings, free from conflict or contrast.

I keep it really simple. I concentrate on being grateful for white gerbera daisies and candle flames. Both assist me in times when my meditation requires a subject of focus. Gerbera daisies and candle flames cause neither conflict nor contrast for me. They exemplify 'clean' in this context. Sit with your subject of gratitude for a while and sink deeper into your body.

Now that you have sat with your subject of gratitude for a few minutes begin to concentrate on the **'feeling'** of gratitude, not the subject of gratitude. Try to maintain this 'feeling state' for an extended period of time, such as 60 seconds. If your mind wanders, gently bring it back to the feeling state of gratitude. Continue doing this until you can maintain the sensation of gratitude for a full 60 seconds.

If you find this difficult try doing it for 10 seconds. There are no rules here! Over time you will get the hang of it.

If this comes easily to you, please feel free to 'string together' 60-second intervals of feeling gratitude. If you are remarkably adept at this process feel free to stay in the feeling state of gratitude for the rest of your life. (Wink!)

Now we will explore the feeling state of Love . . .

# Chapter 12

# Step 2 – Visualization Meditation ~ Feeling Love

# Chapter 12

# Step 2 – Visualization Meditation ~ Feeling Love

We've mastered the feeling state of gratitude. We now move on to Love.

Bring to mind something that you truly love. Again, bring to mind something that you love in a 'clean' way, free from contrast. It won't help bringing to mind the love you have for your daughter when her pig-sty of a room is causing you anxiety.

For me, that would be milk chocolate truffles dusted in cocoa powder. I have only clean feelings of love for this delicacy.

For my friend Kristen, something she truly loves in a clean way is Pinterest. A student of mine is head-over-heels in love with cowboy boots. Concentrate on something that you love, free from conflict or contrast, and then feel into the emotional state just as you did above with gratitude.

You can employ the list of affirmations here if you need help getting to a place of 'clean' love.

- I am awake!
- All is perfect—I am perfect—just as I am, at this moment. All is well.
- I am grateful. I shout my gratitude!
- I choose to be outrageously thankful and fall in love with the knowledge that I am eternally loved.
- I am empowered.
- I feel bold knowing this new reality. I am limitless. My soul is fearless.
- Today, in this moment, I fear not.
- I let go of my projected fear. I choose a new self-image.
- I am whole.
- I come from Love.
- I've got this . . . I am supported.
- I follow the OM Kitty way, the UnTamed way, the Sexy Shakti way. I have nothing to fear. There is nothing to fear. Fear is an

illusion. I am OK with uncertainty. I feel free.

Attempt to be in the feeling of the state of Love for 60 seconds. Practice this just as you did with gratitude.

When you feel confident you know and can experience the feeling states of gratitude and love, it is time to begin the meditation process.

## **Gratitude and Love Meditation:**

Visualize a golden rod of light linking the second chakra with the fourth chakra. Imagine this golden rod of light beginning at the orange colored sacral chakra, running through a field of yellow and linking to the green of the heart chakra. Squeeze Sexy Shakti and let her know you are still engaged.

Allow the feeling state of gratitude and love to flow back and forth along this golden rod. Continue to transmit the energy of the 2$^{nd}$ chakra to the 4$^{th}$ chakra and then reverse the order. Back and forth, allow the energy to mingle and coalesce. Sit for a few minutes envisioning this flow.

You are activating the Divine Alchemy.

Vocalizing at this juncture is often very helpful.

The Sanskrit mantra for the 4th Chakra is Yam (Yummmmmm). Combine the Sacral Chakra mantra Vam with Yam. Repeat throughout as you meditate on the center of your chest. Hug the cynosure, letting Sexy Shakti know you are engaged.

Stay with the emotional state of gratitude and love. If possible, practice this sitting meditation/visualization for 15 minutes daily. Always feel free to extend any meditation as long as you can do so free of concern, worry or feeling conflicted. Something done every day, even for 2 minutes, is better than 60 minutes once a month.

Please remember to breathe in gently and deeply. If you become distracted, consider giving Sexy Shakti another hug.

If you find it helpful, I have included a short audio recording for the Feeling Gratitude and Love Meditation on the resource page.

It is time to incorporate Step 3 of the Divine Alchemy process. Let's go listen to the rhythm of our hearts . . .

# Chapter 13

## Step 3 – Heart Beat Rhythm

*"The goal of life is to make your heartbeat match the beat of the universe, to match your nature with Nature."*

*~ Joseph Campbell*

# Chapter 13

# Step 3 – Heart Beat Rhythm

It is time to incorporate into the process the primordial sound of the beating of your heart. Nothing is as soothing as the rhythmic beat of the heart. Nothing is as life giving as the pulse of the heart. This is a testament to the invincible power of the heart as an organ and its role as gate-master of the energetic portal between heaven and earth.

How often have you stopped to simply just tune into the beating of your amazing, supportive, determined and loyal heart? Considering how much work your heart conducts on your behalf, I urge you to take just a brief moment to contemplate the mystery of this electrical organ, giver of life and conduit of immortal, divine love.

I don't always share this with others, but when I envision my emerald green Heart Chakra, it usually appears as an ancient leather-bound text.

It isn't a green, glowing sphere or orb or Chakra Wheel or spinning disc as might usually be envisioned in Chakra Balancing.

Instead, it morphs into an ancient, sacred bound book. The hard leather cover is the color of cool moss and is tooled like a fine saddle or bag. The book is thick with many chapters. The pages are a very pale green, the color of sea foam. The spine is cracked, and the page leafs are worn and dog-eared. There is a small jeweled lock on this ancient text, similar to what might appear on a treasure chest. It is secure. I am able to open the book mentally. I do not need a key. It unlocks for me magically.

When I sit contemplating my Heart Chakra which looks like a sacred tome written in the far past, it always makes me smile—for I am a writer and nothing could be closer to my heart than a book. This metaphor makes perfect sense to me. My Heart Chakra appears to me as a solid, sturdy yet still fragile and well-loved bound manuscript.

When I peer mentally at my Heart Chakra and meditate on 'my tome,' within minutes the book opens. The jeweled lock springs open and the heavy tooled leather binding falls back. The pages unfurl and lie flat. From the center of the open book deep, green tendrils of vine appear. The tendrils grow quickly and surround the book, engulfing it in a leafy blanket.

This, my friends, is the power of metaphor. Do you ever contemplate the metaphors that miraculously show up in your existence? Metaphors appear in our lives to bring us messages and clues.

Metaphor is a tool our higher conscious uses to decipher meaning and bring clarity.

My soul wants me to know this metaphor intimately. I am the book, and the book is me, solid, sturdy, yet fragile, with many chapters. The book is well loved. There is a magical jeweled lock that springs open upon my command. Once open, the book becomes Divine Love. Yes, I will take that metaphor every day and savor the message it reveals. I urge you to consider doing the same thing as you witness metaphors popping up in your life.

There is peace and serenity that washes over me when I sit and watch my heart chakra. I have personalized each of my energetic centers in a similar way. Please feel free to personalize your seven primary energetic centers as well. There is no telling what your soul wants you to know about yourself through the use of metaphor.

In case you were wondering, my orange colored Sacral Chakra doesn't appear as a piece of fruit. Instead, it appears as a large, salmon hued silky peony. The petals have small drops of dew sprinkled hither and yon.

When I contemplate my Sacral Chakra, many of the petals are still closed in upon each other, as if they are waiting for the lips of the sun to kiss them gently awake. They slowly open, the outer layers first, then the next and the next. Finally, the center of my peony is touched by this bright sun and opens to the warm kiss. It is now ready to be activated, and I focus my meditative attention upon the dwelling place of creation.

As we begin this meditation, please remain still. Continue to see the flow of energy between the $2^{nd}$ chakra and the $4^{th}$ chakra. Continue to watch the energy flow from the orange energetic center through a field of yellow and into the green energetic center.

With the wisdom of your inner being, begin to discern the beating of your heart. Listen to your heart beat. If you cannot hear your heart beating, it may be helpful to visualize the heart beating. If you are still unable to hear your heart beat—you can try out this audio-recording here - (Slow Soothing Heartbeat Sound (1 Hour of ASMR) crysknife007).

With your attention on your heart beat, begin to feel the sensation of the beating. Visualize your heart blanketed in a coat of vibrant green. Just sit silently and watch it pump, listen to it beat, your beautiful heart sitting cozily in a green blanket. Breathe. Watch your heart beat, feel it pulse.

You have set an awesome intention. You have experienced gratitude and love. You have artfully caused the universal life energy to flow back and forth from your $2^{nd}$ chakra to your $4^{th}$ chakra. You have activated the Divine Alchemy and blanketed your sacral chakra in vibrant green. You have watched your heart pump and felt it pulse.

Congratulations. You have now completed the second part of the process.

**True Story #2:**

I once studied under the great 12th-century mystic Lal Arifa for an extended period. She preferred we simply call her Lalla.

While there I met a woman named Raiza. She was devoted to her faith tradition and was well respected as the 'maid servant' to her Lord Vishnu. Raiza immersed her entire being into her devotional worship—known as bhakti.

Although Raiza had lived a life many would consider significant she was broken hearted.

She had been on a road of spiritual enlightenment for many years, but in her heart, she never felt fulfilled. The reason for this was because she inadvertently became caught up in all the untruths contained within her mind.

Raiza was inextricably attached to 'rules' or stories she believed were true about the 'appropriate way to become enlightened.'

Raiza never believed she was devotional enough. She was convinced she was 'never getting it right.' She was further convinced that the road to enlightenment and bliss was through strict adherence to devotion and the dissolving of desire.

Ha! As you can imagine, Raiza had become shriveled, like a dry, dead leaf that has fallen from the Tree of Life.

Raiza had become devoid of all creativity and vitality. She denied her feminine sensuality to the point where she became a frozen, brittle nub. Raiza wasn't loving herself. She had no self-compassion. She had no real passion at all.

Raiza believed she was 'failing.' She wasn't loving herself as Source wants her to love herself. Raiza was in desperate need of Part Two—The Divine Alchemy. She needed to connect her 2nd chakra with the 4$^{th}$ chakra.

Raiza had nothing less than an epiphany when she completed the entirety of Princess Padmaja's process. The once frozen and brittle Raiza realized there is no 'right way or wrong way.' She learned the key was to simply flow. To be. To know contentment. To rest in the knowing, you are eternally supported and loved. There are no rules in awakening.

Friends, there is no 'right' or 'enough' in this process. Just do it, you can't do it wrong, and you'll never finish. It's a lifelong gig.

Raiza later informed me her favorite part of the process was part two—The Divine Alchemy.

"The flow, OM Kitty, the flow was what changed everything for me. When my sacral chakra connected purposefully with my heart chakra, I knew without reservation that I had everything upside down and backward. OM Kitty, you were right—there isn't a 'right way' to do this. I just needed to flow.

# – Part Three –

## Release of the Phoenix

# Chapter 14

# Ignite Your Fire Bird

*"To know the fire, I become the fire. I am power. I am light."*

*~ Egyptian Book of the Dead*

# Chapter 14

# Ignite Your Fire Bird

Part 3 of Padmaja's process relies heavily on the art of visualization and again combines it with the magic of metaphor. As you just learned in Chapter 13, metaphor is an outstanding tool for taking us to a place of immediate awareness. Metaphor can create an 'Aha' moment, unlike any other tool. When combining visualization, metaphor, energy work, and deliberate creation, the result is unparalleled inner awakening.

We want to 'rebirth' ourselves, like the famous Phoenix rising from the ashes.

As with all visualization and deliberate creation, it is critical to set your intention. You will notice this is a theme that runs through all 3 parts of Princess Padmaja's process.

We begin by using the ancient symbol of the Phoenix Rising. This symbol is the ultimate metaphor for rebirth (well . . . except for the metaphor of a cat with 9 lives of course!) It is associated with resurrection and can be used as a tool for your own resurrection and ascension into your real life.

There are many renditions of the Phoenix rising story. Every wisdom culture has its own slant on the meaning and symbolism of the magical bird. Perhaps the most well-known version is derived from the Egyptian translation.

In ancient Egyptian mythology, the Phoenix is a sacred female Firebird, and her plumage consists of radiant gold and red feathers. It is said this bird resembles a Great Blue Heron and lives an extraordinarily long lifetime. When it enters its final stage of this life-cycle, the phoenix builds itself a cozy, sturdy nest of cinnamon twigs which it then ignites. The sacred bird and nest combust and are then reduced to ashes, only to be reborn, stronger, wiser, better. That is one heck of a metaphor!

There is only one step in Part 3 of Padmaja's process.

It is a big step. Actually, it is a big leap. It is a big, fat, juicy metaphorical leap of faith. I know you are ready for this. I believe in you.

I present Part 3 of Padmaja's Process—Release of the Phoenix.


## Let us Rise like a Phoenix!

Begin by becoming still. Picture a golden shaft within you which acts as a channel to flow all that is pure and good. This light shaft is the conduit for Holy Spirit, that which is Pure Benevolent Love. In the Hindu tradition this shaft, or channel, is referred to as Sushumna. This channel runs from the Root Chakra—the Muldahara and extends past the Crown Chakra, the Sahasrara.

We want to quickly activate our entire chakra system before we release the Phoenix.

Begin by visualizing a crystal decanter filled with iridescent, clear liquid. Decant the liquid beginning at the Crown Chakra and visualize this glistening liquid fill this ultra-violet colored space.

Follow the liquid traveling down past the indigo colored ajna, the 3rd Eye Chakra, past the sky-blue throat chakra, and down into the vibrant green heart chakra.

Allow the liquid to pool here in the heart center. Visualize the liquid turning a healthy, pure green. Allow it to swirl around in the Anahatta as it descends from the spiritual energy centers and makes its way down to the earthly energy centers.

You mentally push the green-hued liquid downward, and it returns to its original state of translucency. Follow the clear, glistening liquid as it moves past your golden-yellow solar-plexus chakra, down through your brightly lit up orange sacral chakra and finally comes to rest upon the floor of the deep red root chakra.

Now that you have activated your entire energetic system it is time to call upon the Phoenix.

With your eyes closed, your heart open and your mind clear, begin to visualize a Rising Phoenix. Your Phoenix can be any bird of your choosing. There are no rules here!

Allow your Phoenix to be grand, bigger than life, full of vibrancy. Deck her out in jewels and a crown. Or make her supremely simple and serene. This is your visualization, and you can conjure the Phoenix that most appeals to you.

I once visualized a flaming peony pink flamingo with gold tipped plumage, wearing a diamond choker and a red boa around her neck. This is your Phoenix friends, make her memorable.

Where is your bird? Is she in a silent field of wild flowers? Is she sitting perched on a red rock in the desert? Is she lounging under a palm tree with a mai-tai? Remember, there are no rules.

Make eye contact with your Phoenix. Let her know you are here and that you intend to help her make her pyre and witness her process of rebirth. Let your Phoenix know you will bear witness to her incineration. You will stand fast as she burns to a crisp by her own volition. Let Phoenix know you will remain with her as she re-emerges from the ashes, resurrected and ready for ascension.

Share with your Phoenix that you only have one small request. That she kindly share with you a small egg of her making, which you will ingest.

She will understand that by ingesting the egg, you will take part in the rebirthing process. Phoenix is your friend; she will gladly provide you with a magical egg.

You begin by helping Phoenix gather kindling for the pyre. This process can be as detailed as you like. Whatever you and Phoenix decide is perfect.

Once the pyre is ready, you bow to Phoenix as she climbs on her cozy pyre and prepares for ignition. As she settles down and flattens her plumage, you once again make eye contact. Phoenix looks regal. She knows she is in no danger. She willfully dies to this life and looks forward to rebirth. She burns to *heal*.

She closes her eyes and bows her head, acknowledging your presence. Then, poof, the pyre is engulfed in flames.

What happens during the incendiary process is of your own making. I choose to make the process mystical for my own liking. I do not actually see Phoenix during the incineration. Rather, I see a giant multi-color flame that rises up into the sky and shoots sparks of cosmic energy outward that fall to the ground in streams of pure radiant light.

Suddenly you realize the flames have disappeared and only ashes remain. You walk to the pyre and there like a little gift is one, small, perfect bite-size egg. You silently thank Phoenix for the gift and pop it into your mouth swallowing it whole. You have been bestowed with the magical alchemy that just occurred and have ingested it for safe keeping. It remains with you forever.

The ashes of the pyre begin to swirl. A cloud begins to form. From the cloud of ashes a small, young Phoenix appears. What does she look like? Is she eager and frisky? Is she indestructible? Does she appear to be ready for new explorations?

I tend to imagine this new Phoenix as a young Great Heron. She stands on one leg. She is in perfect balance. She is the Goddess of her Domain.

Phoenix takes flight and leaves you. As you digest your egg the power of transformation spreads throughout your entire physical being. You feel empowered. You feel new. You sense the energy of the alchemy travel to your sacral chakra. Allow the feeling sensation to pound and resonate within your inner orange flame. Let the sensation rise to meet the cynosure and hug Sexy Shakti.

This process of rebirth and renewal will work wonders upon your Sexy Shakti, revitalizing her at any time in any place. Simply recall the 3rd step of the process whenever you feel overwhelmed, unfulfilled, misunderstood or even broken. Use the visualization of your personal Phoenix to ignite your Sexy Shakti whenever you feel depleted.

Become new again.

I want to share a few beautiful excerpts from The Egyptian Book of the Dead: The Book of Going Forth by Day. This text is also interpreted to mean Emerging Forth into the Light.

You can read the entire text here. Listen to what Phoenix Rising has to say and recall these words when you conduct Step 3 of Padmaja's Process.

*"I flew straight out of heaven, a mad bird full of secrets. I came into being as I came into being. I grew as I grew. I changed as I change . . .*

*. . . I am the seed of every god, beautiful as evening, hard as light . . .*

*. . . I will live forever in the fire spun from my own wings. I'll suffer burns that burn to heal. I destroy and create myself like the sun that rises burning from the east and dies burning in the west. To know the fire, I become the fire. I am power. I am light. I am forever. On earth and in heaven I am. This is my body, my work. This is my deliverance.*

*The heat of transformation is unbearable, yet change is necessary. It burns up the useless, the diseased. Time is a cool liquid; it flows away like a river. We shall see no end of it. Generation after generation, I create myself. It is never easy. Long nights I waited, lost in myself, considering the stars. I wage a battle against darkness, against my own ignorance, my resistance to change, my sentimental love for my own folly.*

*. . . There is no end to becoming . . . I change and change again, generation after generation . . .*

*. . . I have entered fire. I become invisible; yet I breathe in the flow of sun, in the eyes of children, in the light that animates the white cliffs at dawn. I am the God in the world in everything, even in darkness. If you have not seen me there, you have not looked. I am the fire that burns you, that burns in you. To live is to die a thousand deaths, but there is only one fire, one eternity."*

As you now know my friends, your job is to become UnTamed. This is the process. Die to your old self. Live a **wild-ish** life. Become the Wayfinder of your one, true life.

I became familiar with the term Wayfinder, after I read a book by Martha Beck, Ph.D., entitled *Finding Your Way in a Wild New World.*

Martha writes "Wayfinders, by definition, create paths where there are none and find destinations no one knew were there."

Don't you want to forge a new path? Isn't that why you want to awaken Sexy Shakti? Living **wild-ishly** is to live creatively and deliberately. That is the entire point of Padmaja's process. When you let the

Phoenix rise, you naturally unleash your inner Wayfinder.

While traveling in Persia during my fourth cat-life, I met a man I will call Jalal.

Jalal was the son of a Sufi scholar. He had attended one of my lectures and sat silently listening. He then left, and I didn't see him again for two years.

One day he found me sitting in a pomegranate orchard. He shared with me that he was on the 'mystic's path.'

"OM Kitty," Jalal said, "I have mastered Padmaja's process."

I replied, "Which part of Padmaja's process did you most favor?"

"Part 3, the Phoenix," he replied.

"Jalal, you are a mystic and are on the healer's path. To be the light you must burn through the darkness. As a healer, a light-worker, you will be watching your Phoenix climb upon that pyre again and again."

"Yes, OM Kitty. I have watched my Phoenix turn to ashes many times. There is no end to **becoming**. My personal bird is a great silver Falcon with jet black eyes and a golden beak."

Jalal came and sat close to me under the pomegranate tree. "Whenever I am experiencing exquisite pain, feeling broken, or I am in despair, I turn to this part of Padmaja's process. I've watched my Phoenix, the Falcon, burn, disintegrate and turn to ash on many occasions. My family is now very familiar with the times I descend into pain, they understand this is the path of the healer. I have said to them many times 'You've watched my despair, now witness my rising.' I urge my loved ones to do the same, but they don't. For some reason, they are not interested."

"Jalal, as a healer, it is your path to shine a light, to encourage and inspire others to release the darkness. However, most will avoid the pyre. They fear the flames. There is nothing you can do about that. They will simply not understand that from the burning death, great beauty will emerge, like the making of a diamond. Not everyone is teachable."

Jalal instinctively knew this to be true. I could tell by the mischievous mix of merriment and wisdom in his eyes.

I asked him "What happens after Falcon dies and is reborn?"

"Upon his rebirth, he leaves me a shiny crystal egg. I consume the egg, and through the alchemy, I transform. Falcon flies away. I know he will return again."

I replied, "It's a journey, Jamal. You are correct; there is no end to **becoming**."

Dear reader, I know part 3 of Padmaja's Process will resonate with you. I know you want to become UnTamed just as I did. I urge you to practice this process over and over.

We have come to the close of Padmaja's Process. But there is still more to Awakening Sexy Shakti, and I share this in Book II.

So far, on this life changing process you have discovered the following:

In part one—Igniting the Flame, you have learned how to find Sexy Shakti and connect with this life giving femasculine energy. You know where your Hot Spot resides and you know how to access it. You have learned to set an intention and manifest your desires for an UnTamed Life. You have stirred Sexy Shakti awake and are ready for new levels in the area of creativity, sensuality, clarity, heightened sexuality, intimate love, empowerment, and vibrancy.

In part two—The Divine Alchemy, you have connected your Heart Chakra with the Sacral

Chakra and understand the potent strength of combining these two energetic centers.

You have learned how to introduce the feeling sensation of gratitude and love into your awareness. You understand these two sensations carry in them the power to transform lives. In fact, they can transform the destiny of our world.

You have become intimately aware of your own rhythmic heartbeat. You have visualized the syncing of your heartbeat to the flow of energy between the 2nd chakra and the 4th chakra. You have also developed an easy process for practicing the tool of self-affirmation.

In part three—Release of the Phoenix, you have conjured your ideal Phoenix. You now have a new best friend. Your Phoenix will be your guide to the process of dying to your old self and resurrecting your new self. Through Phoenix, you have discovered a magical alchemy for transformation.

But—there's more!

The Sacral Chakra—your Orange Flame is the energetic center relating to sexuality.

Sexuality is a hot topic as well as a hot button for many. The mere thought of discussing sexuality causes some to flee in panic.

Then there are the **others**, my sweet, engaged and eager students who want to know how Sexy Shakti can resurrect or reinvigorate their sexual lives. Over the years I have been asked to share my teachings on revving up our natural sexual inclinations.

Mastering your sexual dominion is much more than simply understanding the art of sexuality. A Master understands the traits of Sexy Shakti and develops confidence in this arena. Confidence can be acquired even if you have never been confident about anything in your life.

It is important to point out my friends that this is not about promiscuity or risky behavior. No! Never! Your body is a sacred shrine. Treat it as such.

However, having said that, there are some teachings I want to explain, specifically about Mastering your Sexual Dominion Like a Goddess.

I intended to include these teachings here until it was pointed out by a loved one that this fourth process truly deserved its own short and to the point book.

Please continue your journey by reading *Awakening Your Sexy Shakti—Book II: Mastering Your Sexual Dominion like a Goddess*.

# Chapter 15

# Book I Resources

*"When women reassert their relationship with the wildish nature, they are gifted with a permanent and internal watcher, a knower, a visionary, an oracle . . ."*

*~ Clarissa Pinkola-Estes*

# Chapter 15

# Book I Resources

**Having additional meditation audio recordings have proven to be an effective tool for many.**

**VISIT http://eepurl.com/cVqdYr NOW.**

You will receive the following audio recordings as helpful tools to assist you further in Finding Sexy Shakti and becoming UnTamed.

- Chapter 6—Divine Travel ~ Finding Your Sacred Space Guided Meditation Audio
- Chapter 7—Grounding in Your Sacred Place Guided Meditation Audio

- Chapter 8—Treasure Box Tool Audio
- Chapter 12—Resource – Gratitude and Love Meditation Audio

These resources are all located on the same page and easily accessed by clicking on their blue links. If you are reading the paperback version of this book, you may receive the audio recordings as well! Just copy the link above into your browser.

Namaste!

Your friend,

OM Kitty

# Post-Script~ Awakening
# Sexy Shakti Book I

Dear Reader

You have Awakened Sexy Shakti. Congratulations!

I thank you for being brave and choosing to not only 'step out of the box,' but perhaps dispose of the box and start over entirely, from a fresh, new and awakened vantage point.

**Awakening Sexy Shakti—Book I** is the second book in my 5 book series The OM Kitty Book Series: Spiritual Awakening with a *TWIST*.

My Friend, if you have found benefit, useful tools or enjoyed reading Awakening Sexy Shakti-Book I, may I gratefully request you consider posting an **Amazon Review** or **GoodReads Review**?

Reviews are like Vitamin D, a magical dose of sunshine that helps the book and the author grow and feel supported. It is very touching for a writer to receive reviews and make connection with a reader.

Please be sure to download my **Essential Companion Workbook**, your free gift at http://bit.ly/2jBmE2V-OMKitty-Workbook1, (print version available on Amazon for $9.99)

Also remember to access all the tools and meditation audio recordings on the Resource Page or by visiting http://eepurl.com/cVqdYr.

Be sure to access **Awakening YOUR Sexy Shakti—Book II ~ Mastering Your Sexual Dominion Like a Goddess**. This will be followed by a book, still untitled, designed to help you discover the Super-Power traits of the Empath or Highly Sensitive Person. If you would enjoy being an early reader and join Team OM Kitty, please click here Sarah@SaintLaurentCoaching.com and send a note!

# About the Author

As I've mentioned before, it's really hard for cats to hold pens to write or navigate their way around a keyboard. Fortunately, I'm in tight with Sarah Saint Laurent—my best non-fur friend.

Sarah is a writer, Certified Martha Beck Life Coach, Reiki Master, Energy Healer and Mind Set Specialist.

Here's a little information about Sarah. A former business executive, Sarah specializes in freeing you from mediocrity and helping you find your extraordinary life. She is definitely UnTamed and helps others become wildishly UnTamed too.

Whether you find yourself in the wrong relationship, marriage, job, dress size or other dead-end rut, Sarah will gently steer you on the path to clarity where you discover you have all of the answers; they just need to be uncovered.

Learn to release any and all fear-based thoughts and approval-seeking devices and instead dive deep into your real, joyful life. Using the techniques of visualization, Jungian based dream analysis, spirit-guide journeying and deep listening combined with mindfulness based stress reduction coupled with the mind-body connection model, the power of intention setting and deliberate creation, Sarah can help you develop the life you want to call your own.

If you are dealing with weight and body issues, Divorce, recovering from a relationship with a narcissist or other dark personality, Sarah has developed a program to return you to your rightful place, one of peace, clarity, and empowerment.

Founder of the **Becoming UnTamed coaching program, Second Wind Divorce Coaching** and **The EF-Bomb School** (recovery from narcissistic abuse). You can contact Sarah by visiting www.saintlaurentcoaching.com/contact-me and requesting more information.

# Acknowledgements

I would like to thank the following people for their unwavering support, their giant hearts, and their astute minds. Without this band of loving friends/mentors/readers/heart-sisters, *the Awakening Sexy Shakti Books I and II* would never have been manifested in their current rendition.

A book is only as good as the team that comes together to push the writer up the hill, around the bend and then finally back down the hill.

I thank you and feel honored to have your support:

Julie Cline
Emmanuelle Guerrin
Beth Gager
Lauren Oujiri
Katharine Elliott
Amy Colvin
Carol S.
Sarah S.

Made in the USA
Las Vegas, NV
08 December 2021

36461212R00089